WHO MADE THAT FIRST?

FOOD CREATIONS

FROM HOT DOGS TO ICE CREAM CONES

by Jacqueline A. Ball

Consultant: Daniel H. Franck, Ph.D.

BEARPORT
PUBLISHING COMPANY, INC.

New York, New York

Credits:
Cover and title page, Michelle Barbera (illustrator), Firehorse/istockphoto (pretzel), Lyle Koehnlein/ istockphoto (popcorn); 4, Museum of Natural History; 5(T), CORBIS; 5(B), LWA-Dann Tardif/ CORBIS; 6, White Packert/Photonica/Getty Images; 7(T), Tracy Morgan/Dorling Kindersley/ Getty Images; 7(B), Jean Michel Foujols/zefa/Corbis; 8, David Paul Morris/Getty Images; 9(B), James Baigrie/FoodPix/Getty Images; 10, Brian Hagiwara/FoodPix/Getty Images; 11(T), Dennis O'Clair/ Stone/Getty Images; 11(B), William Gottlieb/CORBIS; 12, Najlah Feanny/CORBIS SABA; 13(T), Joe Raedle/Getty Images; 13(B), Randy Faris/CORBIS; 14, Peter Cade/Iconica/Getty Images; 15(T), AP Photo/Mattoon Journal Gazette, Doug Lawhead; 15(B), David Bebber/Reuters/ Corbis; 16, Mitch Tobias/The Image Bank/Getty Images; 17(T), Dennis Gottlieb/FoodPix/Getty Images; 17(B), Lew Robertson/Foodpix; 18, Seymour Hewitt/Iconica/Getty Images; 19(T), R. Holz/ zefa/Corbis; 19(B), Rusty Hill/FoodPix/Getty Images; 20, John Slater/CORBIS; 21(T), Dynamic Graphics Group/Creatas/Alamy; 21(B), Adam Woolfitt/CORBIS; 22, Peter M. Wilson/CORBIS; 23(T), Ian O'Leary/Stone/Getty Images; 23(B), Chuck Pefley /Alamy; 24, PHOTOTAKE Inc. / Alamy; 25(T), Koichi Kamoshida/Getty Images.

Design and production by Dawn Beard Creative and Octavo Design and Production, Inc.

Library of Congress Cataloging-in-Publication Data

Ball, Jacqueline A.
   Food creations : from hot dogs to ice cream cones / by Jacqueline A. Ball.
      p. cm. — (Which came first?)
   Includes bibliographical references and index.
   ISBN 1-59716-130-6 (library binding) — ISBN 1-59716-137-3 (pbk.)
   1. Food—History—Juvenile literature. I. Title. II. Series.

TX355.B354 2006
641.3009—dc22
                         2005029884

For more information, write to Bearport Publishing Company, Inc., 101 Fifth Avenue, Suite 6R, New York, New York 10003. Printed in the United States of America.

1 2 3 4 5 6 7 8 9 10

Contents

Introduction

Did you know there was a time when people didn't eat ice cream? Why? Ice cream hadn't been invented. Today many people are lucky enough to have a huge choice of delicious foods. Over the years inventors have worked to make food healthier and eating more fun. They've also come up with completely new things to eat.

This book describes ten pairs of food creations. Read about each pair and guess which one came first. Then turn the page for the answer.

▲ Cavemen hunted their own food.

Turn the page to
find out which
came first.

Which Came First?

Peanut Butter

The Incas, a people who lived in South America, used to leave jars of peanuts on graves as food for people after they died. Today, peanut butter is found in many homes. About half of all peanuts grown are used to make this tasty treat.

▲ George Washington Carver discovered 300 different uses for peanuts, including paper, oils, and ink.

The world's largest PB&J sandwich used 150 pounds (68 kg) of peanut butter and 50 pounds (23 kg) of jelly. It was created on November 6, 1993, in Peanut, Pennsylvania.

Jelly

Jelly is made from fruit juice. It comes in many different flavors, including strawberry and raspberry. However, grape jelly is the kind most often found on PB&J sandwiches.

Answer: Peanut Butter

More than 3,000 years ago, the Incas created a paste out of ground peanuts. Then in 1890, a doctor invented the peanut butter we eat today. He wanted his patients to have an easy-to-eat, high-**protein** food.

Jelly was first made in the Middle East around A.D. 1100. It is believed that soldiers brought it back home to Europe.

In 1763, the Fourth Earl of Sandwich put meat between bread slices. He wanted to keep one hand free to play cards while he ate. Little did he know he had just created the first sandwich.

Turn the page to find out which came first.

Which Came First?

Hot Dog

The first hot dogs were actually small sausages. They were often called "dachshund (DAHKS-*hunt*) sausages" because they were shaped just like the dogs.

▲ **A dachshund**

Hamburger

Long ago people ground up beef so it was easier to **digest**. Then they ate it raw. Later, ground beef was cooked. Finally, ground beef patties were made into a sandwich called a hamburger.

Answer: Hot Dog

The first hot dogs were made in 1487 in Frankfurt, Germany. For this reason, they're also known as frankfurters.

The hamburger sandwich was invented between the 1880s and 1900. Four American towns claim to be the place where the hamburger was invented. Most people agree that hamburgers were first served at the 1904 World's Fair in St. Louis, Missouri.

In the time it takes to turn a page in a book, Americans will eat 1,600 hamburgers.

Which Came First?

Turn the page to find out which came first.

Ketchup

The Heinz Company wasn't always known for its ketchup. When the company first started, it sold horseradish. The recipe came from H. J. Heinz's mother.

Salsa

Salsa is a Spanish word that means "sauce." Most of the salsa sold today is made from tomatoes, chili peppers, onions, and spices.

9

Answer: Salsa

The Heinz Company made the first modern ketchup in 1875. These days the company produces more than 1.4 billion bottles of ketchup a year. However, hundreds of years before the Heinz Company made ketchup, Aztec rulers in Mexico ate a mixture of tomatoes, chili peppers, and ground squash. A Spanish writer called it "salsa" for the first time in 1571.

Nachos were invented by a Mexican chef named Ignacio Anaya (ig-NAH-see-oh uh-NYE-uh). His nickname was Nacio, which sounds like *nacho*.

Turn the page to
find out which
came first.

Which Came First?

Canned Food

The first canned food didn't even come in a can. The food was packaged in glass jars. Cans later replaced jars because the glass broke too easily.

Frozen Food

While in the Arctic, Clarence Birdseye saw people quickly freezing the fish they caught. He noticed that when the fish **thawed** it tasted almost the same as fresh fish. He brought this **technique** back to the United States and started selling frozen food in supermarkets.

▲ **Frozen dinners became popular in 1954.**

11

Answer: Canned Food

In 1810, Englishman Peter Durand started making tin-plated iron cans to use as food containers. At the time, it was very **expensive** to can food and only the rich could afford it. More than 100 years later, in 1924, Clarence Birdseye started Birdseye Frozen Seafood. He became known as the "Father of Frozen Food."

Canned food was invented because of a contest held by French Emperor Napoleon Bonaparte. He offered a reward to any inventor who could come up with a way to preserve food.

Which Came First?

Turn the page to find out which came first.

▲ **Milton Hershey started his chocolate company in Derry Church, Pennsylvania. The town was later renamed Hershey in Milton's honor. Today there are many different types of chocolate bars to choose from.**

Chocolate Bar

Chocolate used to be eaten only by rich people. Then Milton Hershey invented a way to make milk chocolate that everyone could enjoy and afford.

Ice Cream Cone

Edible cones weren't always used to hold ice cream. There was a time that cones were made out of paper and metal. Try taking a bite out of that!

Answer: Chocolate Bar

Joseph Fry made the first chocolate bar in England in 1847. Before then, people only drank chocolate.

Edible ice cream cones weren't around until the 1880s. In 1904, ice cream cones were served for the first time in America at the St. Louis World's Fair. An ice cream seller ran out of dishes, so a nearby baker made cone-shaped waffles to hold the frozen treat.

In the mid-1880s, ice cream sold on the streets in England was called "hokey pokey."

Turn the page to find out which came first.

Which Came First?

Bagel

What's the "hole" truth? Some think the word *bagel* comes from the German word for "bend." Others say it comes from a word meaning "ring." Either way, a bagel is made from dough that is boiled and then baked.

▲ **In 1996, this bagel was the world's largest, weighing in at 563 pounds (255 kg).**

Doughnut

The first doughnuts were solid balls or "knots" of fried dough, so they had no holes. They were made by cooks with the dough that was leftover from baking bread.

Answer: Bagel

The first bagels were made in Poland in the 1600s. Doughnuts were introduced in Holland around the same time. However, a sea captain is said to have invented the doughnut hole in 1847 when he stuck a doughnut on a spoke of his ship's wheel.

▲ **Bagels come in many different varieties such as sesame seed, onion, garlic, and pumpernickel.**

Bellysinkers, doorknobs, and burl cakes are all nicknames for doughnuts. Solid doughnuts were called *olykoeks*, or oily cakes, because they were fried in oil.

Which Came First?

Pasta

The average American eats about 20 pounds (9 kg) of pasta every year. People who live in Italy eat three times that much. Dry pasta is made from ground **durum** wheat flour, which has more **nutrients** than white flour.

Pizza

At one time, pizza was sold in the streets of Naples, Italy, for breakfast, lunch, and dinner. The only toppings available were mushrooms and **anchovies**.

Answer: Pasta

Some historians say the **Etruscans** were making pasta in 300 B.C. Yet even earlier, in about 2000 B.C., the Chinese were eating a noodle-like food. This food became **popular** because it was easy to make and **inexpensive**.

Pizza as we know it today was invented in 1889. A chef combined flatbread with tomato sauce, mozzarella cheese, and basil for Italy's Queen Margherita. Pizza Margherita is still popular today.

Thomas Jefferson brought the first macaroni machine to America from France in 1789.

Turn the page to
find out which
came first.

Which Came First?

Breakfast Cereal

The first cold, ready-to-eat breakfast cereal was called *Granula*. Actually it wasn't really ready-to-eat. The nuggets were so hard that they needed to be soaked overnight before anyone could chew them.

◀ **Studies show that kids like to read the cereal box as much as they like to eat the food inside.**

Yogurt

Yogurt contains a healthy **bacteria** that helps your stomach process food. At one time, a scientist even believed that if you ate yogurt regularly, you could live to be 150 years old. However, this idea has proved not to be true.

Answer: Yogurt

Historians believe that yogurt was most likely discovered by accident at least as far back as 2000 B.C. They say milk carried by herdsmen in the mountains probably **curdled** due to the heat of the sun. The herdsmen ate it and liked the tangy taste.

A doctor looking to promote healthy eating created *Granula* in 1863. The cereal contained a lot of **fiber**.

Eat breakfast every day! Some research has shown that students who ate breakfast regularly were less likely to get a cold or the flu.

Which Comes Next?

Here are two new food creations that inventors are working on right now. Which one do you think will hit U.S. supermarkets next?

Square Watermelons

Why would anyone want a square watermelon? It fits better in shipping cartons and the refrigerator. These watermelons are being grown in Japan right now. However, they're very expensive— $82 each.

▲ **Nori, dry seaweed, helps hold sushi together.**

Edible Food Wraps

No need to rewrap food that is sealed with these. They fit around food like plastic wrap or *nori*, the wrappers used in sushi. Edible food wraps are made from very thin sheets of fruits and vegetables.

Scorecard

How many did you get correct?

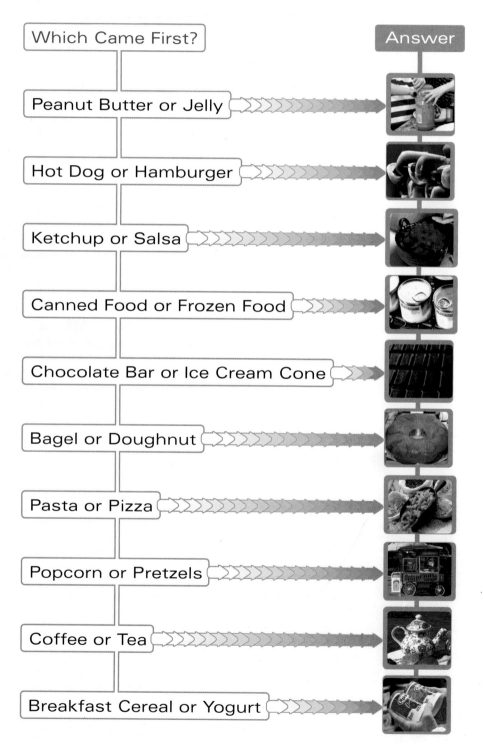

Which Came First?	Answer
Peanut Butter or Jelly	
Hot Dog or Hamburger	
Ketchup or Salsa	
Canned Food or Frozen Food	
Chocolate Bar or Ice Cream Cone	
Bagel or Doughnut	
Pasta or Pizza	
Popcorn or Pretzels	
Coffee or Tea	
Breakfast Cereal or Yogurt	

Bonus Questions

Now you know which of the food creations in this book came first. Here are a few bonus questions.

1. **Ice cream sundaes were invented as a way to serve ice cream sodas without**
   a. whipped cream
   b. soda water
   c. syrup
   d. nuts

2. **Cotton candy is spun sugar. It was first served at**
   a. a state fair
   b. a movie theater
   c. a circus
   d. an amusement park

3. **The same person who invented a lollipop-making machine also invented**
   a. Jell-O
   b. coconut flakes
   c. LifeSavers
   d. chocolate sprinkles

4. **At one time people thought tomatoes were**
   a. rotten
   b. bad-tasting
   c. magical
   d. poisonous

Just the Facts

❋ Frank Epperson invented Popsicles when he was 11 years old. One cold night, he left out a cup of juice, with a stirrer in it, to see how it would taste. In 1923, he started selling his creations. He called them Epsicles. Later, his children renamed the fruit ices Popsicles after what they called him: Pop.

❋ In the United States, National Peanut Butter and Jelly Day is on April 2.

❋ Not all new products and flavors make it on the market. Five Jell-O flavors that failed are celery, coffee, cola, apple, and chocolate.

❋ Pound for pound, a hamburger costs more than a new car.

❋ You can buy hot and cold coffee in cans in Japan.

❋ Pizza Margherita's colors—green, red, and white—are the colors of the Italian flag.

❋ Customers in early English coffeehouses sometimes paid servers a little extra money to get their coffee faster. The money was put in a box labeled "To Insure Promptness." The idea of a tip in a restaurant comes from the initials T.I.P.

The History of Food Creations

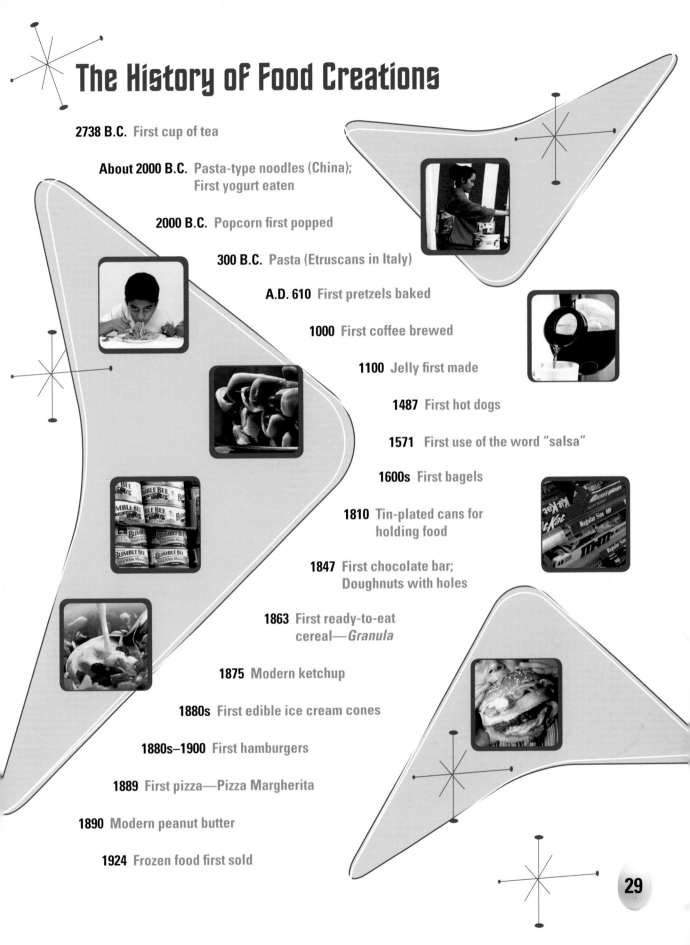

2738 B.C. First cup of tea

About 2000 B.C. Pasta-type noodles (China); First yogurt eaten

2000 B.C. Popcorn first popped

300 B.C. Pasta (Etruscans in Italy)

A.D. 610 First pretzels baked

1000 First coffee brewed

1100 Jelly first made

1487 First hot dogs

1571 First use of the word "salsa"

1600s First bagels

1810 Tin-plated cans for holding food

1847 First chocolate bar; Doughnuts with holes

1863 First ready-to-eat cereal—*Granula*

1875 Modern ketchup

1880s First edible ice cream cones

1880s–1900 First hamburgers

1889 First pizza—Pizza Margherita

1890 Modern peanut butter

1924 Frozen food first sold

Glossary

anchovies (AN-choh-vees) small, salty fish

anthropologists (*an*-thruh-POL-uh-jists) people who study the characteristics, beliefs, and ways of different people around the world

bacteria (bak-TIHR-ee-uh) tiny living things; some bacteria are useful, while others can cause disease

beverages (BEV-rij-iz) drinks

caffeine (kaf-EEN) a chemical often found in soda, coffee, and tea that stimulates the nervous system

curdled (KUR-duhld) when milk goes sour and becomes a solid

digest (dye-JEST) to break down food so that it can be absorbed into a person's blood

durum (DUR-uhm) a type of wheat used in making pasta

edible (ED-uh-buhl) able to be eaten

Etruscans (ih-TRUHS-kuhnz) people who lived in northern and central Italy starting around 800 B.C.

expensive (ek-SPEN-siv) costing a lot of money

fiber (FYE-bur) parts of foods that pass through the body but are not digested

inexpensive (*in*-ik-SPEN-siv) not costing a lot of money

nutrients (NOO-tree-uhnts) food, proteins, vitamins, and minerals that are needed by people to stay healthy

patent (PAT-uhnt) a legal document that gives an inventor the right to sell his or her invention

popular (POP-yuh-lur) liked by many people

protein (PROH-teen) a substance that helps one keep strong and healthy, and is found in meat, cheese, eggs, and fish

scones (SKOHNS) a tea biscuit eaten with either butter or jam

tassels (TASS-uhlz) the silk-like threads found on corn

technique (tek-NEEK) a way of doing something

thawed (THAWD) melted

Bibliography

Ayto, John. *An A-Z of Food & Drink*. New York: Oxford University Press (2002).

Davidson, Alan. *The Oxford Companion to Food*. New York: Oxford University Press (1999).

Kimmerle, Beth. *Candy: The Sweet History*. Portland, OR: Collectors Press (2003).

Wood, Richard, consulting editor. *Great Inventions*. Alexandria, VA: Time-Life Books (1995).

Read More

Bowdish, Lynea. *George Washington Carver*. Danbury, CT: Children's Press (2004).

Casey, Susan. *Kids Inventing: A Handbook for Young Inventors*. Hoboken, N.J.: John Wiley & Sons (2005).

Markle, Sandra. *Chocolate: A Sweet History*. New York: Penguin Putnam Books for Young Readers (2005).

Taylor, Barbara. *I Wonder Why Zippers Have Teeth: and Other Questions About Inventions*. Boston: Kingfisher (2003).

Learn More Online

Visit these Web sites to learn more about food creations:

www.hot-dog.org

www.sturgispretzel.com

Index

About the Author

Jacqueline A. Ball has written and produced more than 100 books for kids and adults. She lives in New York City.